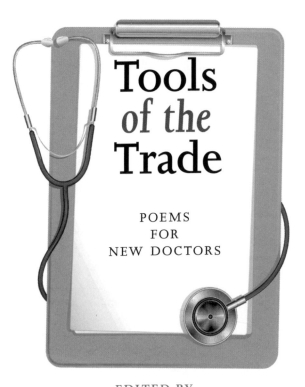

Tools
of the
Trade

POEMS
FOR
NEW DOCTORS

EDITED BY

Lilias Fraser
Dr John Gillies GP
Kate Hendry
Dr Lesley Morrison GP
Revd Ali Newell

Scottish **Poetry** Library

First published in 2016 by
Scottish Poetry Library
5 Crichton's Close
Edinburgh
EH8 8DT
www.scottishpoetrylibrary.org.uk

ISBN 978-0-9562191-9-0

The publisher is grateful for all the donations towards the costs
of this anthology.

Typeset in Stone Print and Carter Sans by Gerry Cambridge
www.gerrycambridge.com
Produced by Productive Production, www.productive.uk.com

Printed and bound in Scotland

CONTENTS

From the Editors
Preface

SECTION I: LOOKING AFTER YOURSELF

SECTION II: LOOKING AFTER OTHERS

SECTION III: BEGINNINGS

SECTION IV: BEING WITH ILLNESS

SECTION V: ENDINGS

FROM THE EDITORS

MANY CONGRATULATIONS ON graduating as a doctor. We hope that you will find your work satisfying and enjoyable.

There will be times when it is also emotionally draining and difficult and, for those times, we offer *Tools of the Trade*, a little book of poetry, a friend to carry with you and consult when you need comfort, inspiration or connection with the outside world. Or when what the poet Mary Oliver calls 'this one wild and precious life' is proving particularly challenging.

Being a doctor is a privilege. You will hear stories that perhaps no one else has ever heard; patients will share their innermost feelings and secrets with you. The art of listening, truly listening, is a precious one; you will learn from patients about their lives, about their illnesses and about yourself.

Art and literature provide invaluable insights into the human condition and what makes us the people we are. The criteria for choosing the poems in this little book were that they were intelligible, short and, in some way, spoke to the experience of being a doctor. Poetry may not initially appeal to everyone. Some of you may be tempted to ignore (or recycle!) the book; we believe that there will be at least one poem in it that will speak to you directly, in which you will recognise yourself or a situation or emotion and find it helpful in some way. So do persist!

To care and be compassionate to others, we first need to be compassionate, to look after, to be kind, to ourselves. To deal with others' stress we need to find ways of coping with our own; keeping as physically, mentally, emotionally well as possible is important. *Tools* may sometimes provide just the right tonic.

This second edition has been generously supported by the Royal College of General Practitioners Scotland and the Medical and Dental Defence Union of Scotland. We are grateful to both. Thanks also to the Scottish Poetry Library under the inspiring leadership of Robyn Marsack for embracing the project so enthusiastically, to Revd Ali Newell, Associate Chaplain at Edinburgh University, and Kate Hendry for their valuable co-editing work, and to Amy McDonald and Lilias Fraser for their care of the project.

So....enjoy the poems, carry them with you, share them with your friends, let us know of any you especially like, or any that we might have included.

Use them as tools to help connect with your patients, your colleagues, yourself.

Dr Lesley Morrison
GP

Dr John Gillies
Chair, RCGP Scotland (2010–2014)

PREFACE

THE BEST CONTEMPORARY poetry is life-affirming and directly relevant to our lives. Pay attention to these poems. Listen to them and reflect on them. Clearly, it is essential that doctors are thoroughly trained in diagnostics and therapeutics—patients expect to meet a doctor with these skills, and rightly so. Reflecting on poetry, and indeed on all the Arts, can produce a different sort of doctor: one who is richer and deeper as an individual; one who sometimes has to deliver the products of scientific advance that will transform people's lives, but who also has the ability to relate to and communicate with people whose lives cannot be transformed, but can be enhanced by support and the palliation of suffering. If you add to the scientific method and evidence-based medicine the stimulation and nurturing of the moral imagination by reflecting on poetry, we will have doctors who will not only have highly tuned clinical skills, but also a more profound understanding of the human condition, and of the psychological and moral subtleties that illness reveals. Attend to these poems: they will enrich both your personal and professional lives.

Dr Brendan Sweeney
Chairman
The Medical and Dental Defence Union of Scotland

I

LOOKING AFTER YOURSELF

TOOLS OF THE TRADE *Martin MacIntyre*

New doctors will be empowered by poems
in the pockets of their metaphorical white coats.
There at the ready:
on early, sweaty, scratchy, ward rounds
to deploy while waiting patiently for the consultant's
    late appraisal;
give filing, phlebotomy and form-filling an edge
    and depth;
sweeten tea-breaks as if with juxtaposed Jaffa Cakes
to answer that persistent bleep—while sneaking a pee,
to travel the manic crash and flat-lined emptiness of
    cardiac arrest
thole the inevitability of the inevitable;
to pace with careful cadence;
stop and breathe usefully
arrive ready not to recite by rote;
to be alone with on the boisterous bus home
to txt anxious Mums and Dads—'Are you remembering
    to feed yourself?'
'YES. LOL. Smiley-face—perhaps a frog?'
to place strategically on the cup-ringed cabinet—first
    night on-call,
thrust under the sun-torn pillow on the morning
    following the first night on-call
find undisturbed, but at a different verse, following the
    jumpy party, following the first night on-call

to steal insights into the science of nurses' smiles
to prepare for change.
To take a full history, examine closely and reach a
    working diagnosis: 'You are a human being.'
     'The stars sing as whitely as the mountains.'
To investigate with prudence.
To reconsider the prognosis in the light of better-quality
    information.
To appreciate; pass on; ponder
challenge, relinquish,
allow, accept
be accosted by dignity.
To forgive and free.

*Martin MacIntyre (b. 1965) is a Scottish poet, novelist, storyteller
and doctor who writes in English and Gaelic.*

THE DOOR   *Miroslav Holub*

Go and open the door.
　　　　Maybe outside there's
　　　　a tree, or a wood,
　　　　a garden,
　　　　or a magic city.

Go and open the door.
　　　　Maybe a dog's rummaging.
　　　　Maybe you'll see a face,
or an eye,
or the picture
　　　　of a picture.

Go and open the door.
　　　　If there's a fog
　　　　it will clear.

Go and open the door.
　　　　Even if there's only
　　　　the darkness ticking,
　　　　even if there's only
　　　　the hollow wind,
　　　　even if
　　　　　　nothing
　　　　　　　is there,
go and open the door.

At least
there'll be
a draught.

Miroslav Holub (1923–1998) was a Czech poet and immunologist.

THE GUEST HOUSE *Jelaluddin Rumi translated by*
Coleman Barks

This being human is a guest house.
Every morning a new arrival.

A joy, a depression, a meanness,
some momentary awareness comes
as an unexpected visitor.

Welcome and entertain them all!
Even if they're a crowd of sorrows,
who violently sweep your house
empty of its furniture,
still, treat each guest honorably.
He may be clearing you out
for some new delight.

The dark thought, the shame, the malice,
meet them at the door laughing,
and invite them in.

Be grateful for whoever comes,
because each has been sent
as a guide from beyond.

THE PEACE OF WILD THINGS *Wendell Berry*

When despair for the world grows in me
and I wake in the night at the least sound
in fear of what my life and my children's lives may be,
I go and lie down where the wood drake
rests in his beauty on the water, and the great heron feeds.
I come into the peace of wild things
who do not tax their lives with forethought
of grief. I come into the presence of still water.
And I feel above me the day-blind stars
waiting with their light. For a time
I rest in the grace of the world, and am free.

AH, NOT TO BE CUT OFF *Rainer Maria Rilke*
translated by Stephen Mitchell

Ah, not to be cut off,
not through the slightest partition
shut out from the law of the stars.
The inner—what is it?
if not the intensified sky,
hurled through with birds and deep
with the winds of homecoming.

GIFT *Czesław Miłosz*

A day so happy.
Fog lifted early, I worked in the garden.
Hummingbirds were stopping over honeysuckle flowers.
There was no thing on earth I wanted to possess.
I knew no one worth my envying him.
Whatever evil I had suffered, I forgot.
To think that once I was the same man did not embarrass me.
In my body I felt no pain.
When straightening up, I saw the blue sea and sails.

From **DISENCHANTMENTS**   *Douglas Dunn*

Mineral loneliness. The hour of stone.
A boat cut loose. Not much to steer it with.
Grey branches hanging over Acheron.

Look to the living, love them, and hold on.

BEANNACHT / BLESSING *John O'Donohue*

for Josie, my mother

On the day when
the weight deadens
on your shoulders
and you stumble,
may the clay dance
to balance you.

And when your eyes
freeze behind
the grey window
and the ghost of loss
gets in to you,
may a flock of colours,
indigo, red, green
and azure blue,
come to awaken in you
a meadow of delight.

When the canvas frays
in the currach of thought
and a stain of ocean

blackens beneath you,
may there come across the waters
a path of yellow moonlight
to bring you safely home.

May the nourishment of the earth be yours,
may the clarity of light be yours,
may the fluency of the ocean be yours,
may the protection of the ancestors be yours.

And so may a slow
wind work these words
of love around you,
an invisible cloak
to mind your life.

From 'AN EPISTLE TO JOHN LAPRAIK' *Robert Burns*

Gie me ae spark o' nature's fire,
That's a' the learning I desire;
Then tho' I drudge thro' dub an' mire
                At pleugh or cart,
My muse, tho' hamely in attire,
                May touch the heart.

CATCHING UP ON SLEEP *Roger McGough*

i go to bed early
to catch up on my sleep
                              but my sleep
is a slippery customer
it bobs and weaves
                      and leaves
me exhausted. It
side steps my clumsy tackles.
with ease. Bed
raggled I drag
myself to my knees.

The sheep are countless
I pretend to snore
yearn for chloroform
or a sock on the jaw
body sweats heart beats
there is Panic in the Sheets
until
as dawn slopes up the stairs
to set me free
unawares
sleep catches up on me.

POEM FOR A HOSPITAL WALL *Diana Hendry*

Love has been loitering
down this corridor
has been seen
chatting up out-patients
spinning the wheels of wheelchairs
fluttering the pulse of the night nurse
appearing, disguised, as a bunch of grapes and a smile
hiding in dreams
handing out winds in orthopaedics
adding a wee drappie
aphrodisiaccy
to every prescription.
No heart is ever by-passed by Love.

Love has been loitering down this corridor
is highly infectious
mind how you go. If you smile
you might catch it.

Diana Hendry (b. 1941) is a poet and children's author.
She was the first writer-in-residence at Dumfries and Galloway
Royal Infirmary in 1997–98.

THE BONNIE BROUKIT BAIRN *Hugh MacDiarmid*

Mars is braw in crammasy,
Venus in a green silk goun,
The auld mune shak's her gowden feathers,
Their starry talk's a wheen o' blethers,
Nane for thee a thochtie sparin',
Earth, thou bonnie broukit bairn!
—*But greet, an' in your tears ye'll droun*
The haill clanjamfrie!

crammasy	*crimson*
wheen o' blethers	*pack of nonsense*
broukit	*neglected*
haill clanjamfrie	*whole crowd of them*

To every thing there is a season, and a time to every
    purpose under the heaven:
A time to be born, and a time to die; a time to plant, and
    a time to pluck up that which is planted;
A time to kill, and a time to heal; a time to break down,
    and a time to build up;
A time to weep, and a time to laugh; a time to mourn, and
    a time to dance;
A time to cast away stones, and a time to gather stones
    together; a time to embrace, and a time to refrain
    from embracing;
A time to get, and a time to lose; a time to keep, and a time
    to cast away;
A time to rend, and a time to sew; a time to keep silence,
    and a time to speak;
A time to love, and a time to hate; a time of war, and a
    time of peace.

PSALM EIGHTY-EIGHT BLUES   *Diana Hendry*

Lord, when I'm speechless
when something—not just sorrow
but under that—a dull, numb, nameless dreich
about the heart I hardly seem to have,
when this afflicts me,
when hope's been cancelled,
when the pilot light of me's put out,
when every reflex and response
has been extinguished,

send word, snowdrop, child, light.

II

LOOKING AFTER OTHERS

A MEDICAL EDUCATION *Glenn Colquhoun*

for Dr Peter Rothwell

In obstetrics I learnt that a woman opens swiftly like an
    elevator door.
The body wriggles free like people leaving an office on a wet
    afternoon.

In medicine I learnt that the body is the inside of a watch.
We hunch carefully over tables with blunt instruments.

In paediatrics I learnt that the body is a bird.
I leave small pieces of bread in fine trails.

In geriatrics I saw that the neck becomes the shape of an
    apple core.

In intensive care I discovered that the body is a number.
The sick sweat like schoolboys studying maths before a test.

In orthopaedics I found that the body can be broken.
Bones make angles under skin as though they were part of
    a collapsed tent.

In anaesthetics I saw people hang on narrow stalks like
    ripe apples.

But in the delivery suite I learnt to swear.

*Glenn Colquhoun (b. 1964) is a New Zealand poet, children's writer
and GP.*

From **A YEAR AND A DAY:**
19 OCTOBER 1979–19 OCTOBER 1980
Gael Turnbull

To be taken in small doses as required

October

25: Miss G——, born while Queen Victoria was still alive, standing proudly in the middle of her sitting room in front of a blazing fire, big school-girl grin on her face: 'It's stomach trouble! I'm a terror for stomach trouble.'

November

19: Not yet thirty, her bones full of metastatic breast cancer, so painful she can't bear to be touched, and her two year old son can't understand why his mother won't let him hug her any more.

January

29: 'My husband is all crumbling up.'

30: 'Thank you for listening, doctor. I likes to unravel a bit.'

June

1: 'All blind inside my head if you take my meaning.'

4: Behind the Surgery car park, a blush of roses and on the lawn, a milky way of daisies.

5: 'Threw a coat at him as there wasn't a saucepan handy.'

6: Hailstones in the sunshine, bouncing on the pavement like pearls from a broken necklace.

15: 'If you want my considered judgement: he's pissed.'

October

1: 'My head is full of little men with needles and I feel like one hundred and nine.'

2: His tie stiff with grease and traces of food and pinned to his shirt with a safety pin... asking for 'something to make me go, proper!'

12: Clouds like shreds of sheep wool stuck on a gorse bush, blown and bleached by the sun and the rain... then dabbed with scarlet and magenta.

14: In a little brown gnome hat, puffing and blowing, head almost completely sunk between his shoulders, helped along by a plum pudding wife... his mouth stretched in a permanent grin, one tooth showing.

Gael Turnbull (1928–2004) worked as a GP and anaesthetist in Canada, California and the UK, all the time writing poetry and introducing writers from America, Canada and Britain to each other through his 'Migrant' Press.

NIGHT SISTER *Elizabeth Jennings*

How is it possible not to grow hard,
To build a shell around yourself when you
Have to watch so much pain, and hear it too?
Many you see are puzzled, wounded; few
Are cheerful long. How can you not be scarred?

To view a birth or death seems natural,
But these locked doors, these sudden shouts and tears
Graze all the peaceful skies. A world of fears
Like the ghost-haunting of the owl appears.
And yet you love that stillness and that call.

You have a memory for everyone;
None is anonymous and so you cure
What few with such compassion could endure.
I never met a calling quite so pure.
My fears are silenced by the things you've done.

We have grown cynical and often miss
The perfect thing. Embarrassment also
Convinces us we cannot dare to show
Our sickness. But you listen and we know
That you can meet us in our own distress.

From **PLAYING GOD**   *Glenn Colquhoun*

10. *A note of warning to patients when all else fails*

Sometimes the needle is too blunt.
The stethoscope is too quiet.
The scalpel will not cut.
The scissors chew like old men's gums.

Sometimes the book has not been written.
The pill cannot be swallowed.
The crutches are too short.
The x-rays hide like dirty windows.

Sometimes the thermometer will not rise.
The plaster will not stick.
The stitches cannot hold.
The heart conducts a normal ECG.

Then I have to ask you what to do

Which is what you might
have wanted all along.

JACKSON SPANDER *K.D. Beernink*

Acute and chronic bronchitis

He hadn't the wits to show me signs
Like his friend had done
To convince me he was crazy enough to be committed,
Just for the winter.

He hadn't the courage to say he was famished
That his bedsore was oozing stinking pus
That he didn't have the strength to ride the boxcar
To Pensacola this year
That he thought he was afraid of dying
On a park bench.

He didn't even know that he was asking me to take care of him:
'Hell, Doc, I was takin care of myself
Before your Daddy had fuzz on his chin!'
And when he laughed he hacked his bloody phlegm
Through a toothless, smelly grin
And filled his paper cup.

But he spent that winter on my ward
In the V.A. hospital.

Kenneth Dale Beernink (1938–1969) was an American poet and doctor. His one collection of poems, Ward Rounds, *was published posthumously.*

From DOING CALLS ON THE OLD PORTPATRICK ROAD *Iain Bamforth*

12. *Graham's Landing*
'The ear says more
Than any tongue'

I thought I spoke the language
asking what the matter was, the wrong.
I only wanted to know your history
framed in the window of our time.

Which of us should have first say?
One who inhaled the long firth,
one who seemed a slow-island-Joe,
one who clambered the bare scree up—

The house put on its afternoon disguise,
wrong way round and inside out.
Language was an unreliable hidey-hole
for two social beasts in harness:

me, losing track of the unreliable words
called bait and purchase, you
dangling them in the cold blue sound
that wandered past the window.

*Iain Bamforth (b. 1959) trained as a GP in Galloway. He now lives
in Strasbourg where he writes and thinks about medicine.*

A BRIEF FORMAT TO BE USED WHEN CONSULTING WITH PATIENTS *Glenn Colquhoun*

The patient will talk.

The doctor will talk.

The doctor will listen while
the patient is talking.

The patient will listen while
the doctor is talking.

The patient will think that the doctor
knows what the doctor is talking about.

The doctor will think that the patient
knows what the patient is talking about.

The patient will think that the doctor
knows what the patient is talking about.

The doctor will think that the patient
knows what the doctor is talking about.

The doctor will be sure.
The patient will be sure.

The patient will be sure.
The doctor will be sure.

Shouldn't hurt a bit, should it?

From WILHELM MEISTERS LEHRJAHRE /
WILHELM MEISTER'S APPRENTICESHIP:
'WHEN WE TAKE PEOPLE MERELY THE WAY
THEY ARE...'

Johann Wolfgang Von Goethe, translated by Iain Bamforth

'Wenn wir die Menschen nur nehmen, wie sie sind, so
machen wir sie schlechter; wenn wir sie behandeln, als
wären sie, was sie sein sollten, so bringen wir sie dahin,
wohin sie zu bringen sind.'

'When we take people merely the way they are we make
them worse than they are; when we treat them as if they
were already what they should be, then we make them
everything they could be.'

THE PRECIOUS 10 MINUTES *Hamish Whyte*
for I.D.

The GP stands at the door of his room,
shakes my hand, asks me how I am.
I always smile and say fine, except for...
this niggling problem
or I'm just here for a checkup
or a repeat prescription
or something.

He listens.
He's a cautious man, gets me tested
just in case: 'Let's be sure.'

He sounds me out about an ongoing condition:
if I can live with it
he can live with it.
'As long as you can do the things
you want to do.'
He knows I'm a worrier.

I don't feel rushed.
It's a conversation.
It all seems as it should be.

THESE ARE THE HANDS   *Michael Rosen*

for the 60th anniversary of the NHS

These are the hands
That touch us first
Feel your head
Find the pulse
And make your bed.

These are the hands
That tap your back
Test the skin
Hold your arm
Wheel the bin
Change the bulb
Fix the drip
Pour the jug
Replace your hip.

These are the hands
That fill the bath
Mop the floor
Flick the switch
Soothe the sore
Burn the swabs

Give us a jab
Throw out sharps
Design the lab.

And these are the hands
That stop the leaks
Empty the pan
Wipe the pipes
Carry the can
Clamp the veins
Make the cast
Log the dose
And touch us last.

III

BEGINNINGS

A TIGHT-ROPE ACT *Gael Turnbull*

Holding our breath
in apprehension,
we grasp life.

From **ULTRASOUND**   *Kathleen Jamie*

for Duncan

i. *Ultrasound*

Oh whistle and I'll come to ye,
my lad, my wee shilpit ghost
summonsed from tomorrow.

Second sight,
a seer's mothy flicker,
an inner sprite:

this is what I see
with eyes closed;
a keek-aboot among secrets.

If Pandora
could have scanned
her dark box,

and kept it locked—
this ghoul's skull, punched eyes
is tiny Hope's,

hauled silver-quick
in a net of sound,
then, for pity's sake, lowered.

TWENTY-EIGHT WEEKS *Lesley Glaister*

We nearly missed her.
This little storm of life
could have blown by
before we weathered her.
But here she is: sturdy,
definite, pointing her finger
for *this* and *this* and *more*
and more and more.

TEDDY   *Glenn Colquhoun*

for a child with leukaemia

Teddy was not well.
Teddy had been feeling sick.
Teddy had to go to hospital.
Teddy was told that he had too much blood.
Teddy did not miss his friends.
Teddy knew the thermometer was not sharp.
Teddy was not scared of needles.
Teddy said the medicine would make him better.
Teddy closed his eyes at night.
Teddy ate his vegetables.

Teddy's small girl lay in the corner of his bed.
She was not so sure.
Her eyes were made from round buttons.
The fluff on the top of her head was worn
as though it had been chewed.

ADAM, THERE ARE ANIMALS *Chloe Morrish*

There is a small fox
slipping through the fabric of morning,
still coated in a layer of grey dusk

and carefully placing his paws
between what's left of night
in the garden.

There is a monkey,
a stained toy, in your hand
when you arrive at the hospital,

which none of the fussing people
had noticed
and you had clung to.

There are wild-eyed soldiers' horses,
charging at us from the jigsaw pieces
in the waiting room

where we try to sleep
on the table and chairs
and pretend we're not waiting.

There are several pigeons
on the window ledge, shuffling about
before the steel chimneys and pinking sky

and a seagull's bark
in the deflated quiet
just after you die.

There is an overfed cat
in the arms of a nurse who smokes
by the automatic doors

and there are baby rabbits
eating the grass verges
of the hospital car park.

There is our dog
at the door, confused
when we get home without you.

And on the kitchen table we sit at, dazed
and not quite real, with cups of tea to hold on to,
there is a small plastic horse.

MY PAPA'S WALTZ *Theodore Roethke*

The whiskey on your breath
Could make a small boy dizzy;
But I hung on like death:
Such waltzing was not easy.

We romped until the pans
Slid from the kitchen shelf;
My mother's countenance
Could not unfrown itself.

The hand that held my wrist
Was battered on one knuckle;
At every step you missed
My right ear scraped a buckle.

You beat time on my head
With a palm caked hard by dirt,
Then waltzed me off to bed
Still clinging to your shirt.

DAUGHTER *Ellen Bryant Voigt*

There is one grief worse than any other.

When your small feverish throat clogged, and quit,
I knelt beside the chair on the green rug
and shook you and shook you,
but the only sound was mine shouting you back,
the delicate curls at your temples,
the blue wool blanket,
your face blue,
your jaw clamped against remedy—

how could I put a knife to that white neck?
With you in my lap,
my hands fluttering like flags,
I bend instead over your dead weight
to administer a kiss so urgent, so ruthless,
pumping breath into your stilled body,
counting out the rhythm for how long until
the second birth, the second cry
oh Jesus that sudden noisy musical inhalation
that leaves me stunned
by your survival.

IV

BEING WITH ILLNESS

RECOVERY ROOM   *Patricia Beer*

The noise in the recovery room
Was half footfall and half hum

Like a well-mannered gallery
Of pictures that I could not see.

And then a name disrupted it:
The hated name of childhood: Pat,

A name I had not answered to
For fifty years and would not now.

Another voice began to talk:
Pat. And still I did not speak.

My husband waited in my room
And in the end they sent for him,

After an hour or two of this.
I heard Patricia. And said 'Yes?'

MULTIPLE SCLEROSIS *Cynthia Huntington*

For ten years I would not say the name.
I said: episode. Said: setback, incident,
exacerbation—anything but be specific
in the way this is specific, not a theory
or description, but a diagnosis.
I said: muscle, weakness, numbness, fatigue.
I said vertigo, neuritis, lesion, spasm.
Remission. Progression. Recurrence. Deficit.

But the name, the ugly sound of it, I refused.
There are two words. The last one means: scarring.
It means what grows hard, and cannot be repaired.
The first one means: repeating, or myriad,
consisting of many parts, increasing in number,
happening over and over, without end.

From 'ADDRESS TO THE UNCO GUID' *Robert Burns*

See Social-life and Glee sit down
All joyous and unthinking,
Till, quite transmugrify'd, they're grown
Debauchery and Drinking :
O, would they stay to calculate,
Th' eternal consequences,
Or—your more dreaded hell to state—
Damnation of expenses!

THINGS   *Fleur Adcock*

There are worse things than having behaved foolishly
    in public.
There are worse things than these miniature betrayals,
committed or endured or suspected; there are worse things
than not being able to sleep for thinking about them.
It is 5 a.m. All the worse things come stalking in
and stand icily about the bed looking worse and worse
    and worse.

NOW WHERE? *Jane Kenyon*

It wakes when I wake, walks
when I walk, turns back when I
turn back, beating me to the door.

It spoils my food and steals
my sleep, and mocks me, saying,
'Where is your God now?'

And so, like a widow, I lie down
after supper. If I lie down
or sit up it's all the same:

the days and nights bear me along.
To strangers I must seem
alive. Spring comes, summer;

cool clear weather; heat, rain....

X-RAY *Dannie Abse*

Some prowl sea-beds, some hurtle to a star
and, mother, some obsessed turn over every stone
or open graves to let that starlight in.
There are men who would open anything.

Harvey, the circulation of the blood,
and Freud, the circulation of our dreams,
pried honourably and honoured are
like all explorers. Men who'd open men.

And those others, mother, with diseases
like great streets named after them: Addison,
Parkinson, Hodgkin—physicians who'd arrive
fast and first on any sour death-bed scene.

I am their slowcoach colleague, half afraid,
incurious. As a boy it was so: you know how
my small hand never teased to pieces
an alarm clock or flensed a perished mouse.

And this larger hand's the same. It stretches now
out from a white sleeve to hold up, mother,
your X-ray to the glowing screen. My eyes look
but don't want to; I still don't want to know.

Dannie Abse (1923–2014) was a Welsh poet and chest consultant.

IATROGENIC *Rafael Campo*

You say, 'I do this to myself.' Outside,
my other patients wait. Maybe snow falls;
we're all just waiting for our deaths to come,
we're all just hoping it won't hurt too much.
You say, 'It makes it seem less lonely here.'
I study them, as if the deep red cuts
were only wounds, as if they didn't hurt
so much. The way you hold your upturned arms,
the cuts seem aimed at your unshaven face.
Outside, my other patients wait their turns.
I run gloved fingertips along their course,
as if I could touch pain itself, as if
by touching pain I might alleviate
my own despair. You say, 'It's snowing, Doc.'
The snow, instead of howling, soundlessly
comes down. I think you think it's beautiful;
I say, 'This isn't all about the snow,
is it?' The way you hold your upturned arms,
I think about embracing you, but don't.
I think, 'We do this to ourselves.' I think
the falling snow explains itself to us,
blinding, faceless, and so deeply wounding.

Rafael Campo (b. 1964) is an American poet, essayist and doctor.

STROKE HAIKU *Helen Price*

When a door closes
many small windows open

tiny chinks of light

THE UNPROFESSIONALS *U.A. Fanthorpe*

When the worst thing happens,
That uproots the future,
That you must live for every hour of your future,

They come,
Unorganised, inarticulate, unprofessional;

They come sheepishly, sit with you, holding hands,
From tea to tea, from Anadin to Valium,
Sleeping on put-you-ups, answering the phone,
Coming in shifts, spontaneously,

Talking sometimes,
About wallflowers, and fishing, and why
Dealing with Kleenex and kettles,
Doing the washing up and the shopping,

Like civilians in a shelter, under bombardment,
Holding hands and sitting it out
Through the immortality of all the seconds,
Until the blunting of time.

In order to write, U.A. Fanthorpe abandoned a career in education and became an NHS hospital clerk, an experience that pitchforked her into poetry. In 2002 she was awarded the Queen's Gold Medal for Poetry.

WARD 64 *Sarah Broom*

the curtain's beige and orange checks
do nothing to divide us

when her drip beeps I think it's mine

when she hears the bad news
I have to put my iPod on to keep it out

across the room he's lost his wedding ring
because he's got so thin

skinny fingers
I'd better watch out for that

there is poetry all over the walls
of oncology

and I want to get out

TO MY SURGEON *Valerie Gillies*

No-one else sees me
drowning in the white wave
sprinkled with a terrible salt

invasive lobular carcinoma
is difficult to identify

but you take one look
and I am

held
by your hand
saving my life

V

ENDINGS

THE OLD LADY *Iain Crichton Smith*

Autumn, and the nights are darkening.
The old lady tells us of her past once more.
She muses on the days she spent nursing

at ten shillings a month. 'And what exams!
I could understand anything in those days.
What summers we had then, what lovely autumns.'

And so I imagine her cycling to her work
among the golden leaves, down avenues,
to hospitals which were disciplined and stark

with hard-faced matrons, doctors jovial
with an authority that was never quizzed,
while grizzled Death suckled at his phial,

and autumn glowed and died, outside the ward,
and girlishly she saw it fade in red
in sky and sheet, and evening was barred
with strange sweet clouds that hung above the bed.

HIS STILLNESS *Sharon Olds*

The doctor said to my father, 'You asked me
to tell you when nothing more could be done.
That's what I'm telling you now.' My father
sat quite still, as he always did,
especially not moving his eyes. I had thought
he would rave if he understood he would die,
wave his arms and cry out. He sat up,
thin, and clean, in his clean gown,
like a holy man. The doctor said,
'There are things we can do which might give you time,
but we cannot cure you.' My father said,
'Thank you.' And he sat, motionless, alone,
with the dignity of a foreign leader.
I sat beside him. This was my father.
He had known he was mortal. I had feared they would
    have to
tie him down. I had not remembered
he had always held still and kept quiet to bear things,
the liquor a way to keep still. I had not
known him. My father had dignity. At the
end of his life his life began
to wake in me.

MUM *Arthur Cochrane*

We sat together in silence.
The lost look in your eyes.
Once they were like eternal stars.

You were full of joy and love.
But now is pain and loneliness,
Lost in your own world.

You cry out *Mum*.
But she has been gone some
Twenty years.

You cry out *Mum*.
I pray for the kiss of death to come.
My love.

NOTHING *Selima Hill*

Because she is exhausted
and confused,

and doesn't want to argue,
and can't speak,

she dreams of nothing
for a thousand years,

or what the nurses cheerfully call
a week.

ALZHEIMER'S *Bob Hicok*

Chairs move by themselves, and books.
Grandchildren visit, stand
new and nameless, their faces' puzzles
missing pieces. She's like a fish

in deep ocean, its body made of light.
She floats through rooms, through
my eyes, an old woman bereft
of chronicle, the parable of her life.

And though she's almost a child
there's still blood between us:
I passed through her to arrive.
So I protect her from knives,

stairs, from the street that calls
as rivers do, a summons to walk away,
to follow. And dress her,
demonstrate how buttons work,

when she sometimes looks up
and says my name, the sound arriving
like the trill of a bird so rare
it's rumored no longer to exist.

SECOND OPINION *Douglas Dunn*

We went to Leeds for a second opinion.
After her name was called,
I waited among the apparently well
And those with bandaged eyes and dark spectacles.

A heavy mother shuffled with bad feet
And a stick, a pad over one eye,
Leaving her children warned in their seats.
The minutes went by like a winter.

They called me in. What moment worse
Than that young doctor trying to explain?
'It's large and growing.' 'What is?' 'Malignancy.'
'Why *there*? She's an artist!'

He shrugged and said, 'Nobody knows.'
He warned me it might spread. 'Spread?'
My body ached to suffer like her twin
And touch the cure with lips and healing sesames.

No image, no straw to support me—nothing
To hear or see. No leaves rustling in sunlight.
Only the mind sliding against events
And the antiseptic whiff of destiny.

Professional anxiety—
His hand on my shoulder
Showing me to the door, a scent of soap,
Medical fingers, and his wedding ring.

WHAT THE DOCTOR SAID *Raymond Carver*

He said it doesn't look good
he said it looks bad in fact real bad
he said I counted thirty-two of them on one lung before
I quit counting them
I said I'm glad I wouldn't want to know
about any more being there than that
he said are you a religious man do you kneel down
in forest groves and let yourself ask for help
when you come to a waterfall
mist blowing against your face and arms
do you stop and ask for understanding at those moments
I said not yet but I intend to start today
he said I'm real sorry he said
I wish I had some other kind of news to give you
I said Amen and he said something else
I didn't catch and not knowing what else to do
and not wanting him to have to repeat it
and me to have to fully digest it
I just looked at him
for a minute and he looked back it was then
I jumped up and shook hands with this man who'd just
         given me
something no one else on earth had ever given me
I may have even thanked him habit being so strong

From CUMHA CHALUIM IAIN MHICGIL-EAIN /
ELEGY FOR CALUM I. MACLEAN

Somhairle MacGill-Eain / Sorley MacLean

Tha an saoghal fhathast àlainn
ged nach eil thu ann.
Is labhar an Uibhist a' Ghàidhlig
ged tha thusa an Cnoc Hàllainn
is do bhial gun chainnt

The world is still beautiful
though you are not in it,
Gaelic is eloquent in Uist
though you are in Hallin Hill
and your mouth without speech

WHITE BASIN *Lindy Barbour*

It came to the point that she was weak—
past climbing stairs and in the mornings
had to wash using the kitchen sink.

I went down Castle Street to Wallace Hughes,
Electrical and Hardware, to buy a bowl. The dark shop
smelled as always of paraffin and bare boards.

The bowl was cheap—a simple hemisphere
of thin white plastic with a rolled rim
as white and round as the full moon.

Each morning I held her upright as her white hands swam
like little fishes through the warm water. The garden
was still flowering strongly that November. I watched
her gaze at the roses through two layers of glass.

I kept the bowl and use it now for ordinary things:
handwashing and catching drips. It's as beautiful
as the moon, or as a marble basin of clear water
with fish swimming in moonlight in the dark garden.

From CLEARANCES *Seamus Heaney*

In the last minutes he said more to her
Almost than in all their life together.
'You'll be in New Row on Monday night
And I'll come up for you and you'll be glad
When I walk in the door...Isn't that right?'
His head was bent down to her propped-up head.
She could not hear but we were overjoyed.
He called her good and girl. Then she was dead,
The searching for a pulsebeat was abandoned
And we all knew one thing by being there.
The space we stood around had been emptied
Into us to keep, it penetrated
Clearances that suddenly stood open.
High cries were felled and a pure change happened.

GOING WITHOUT SAYING   *Bernard O'Donoghue*

i.m. Joe Flynn

It is a great pity we don't know
When the dead are going to die
So that, over a last companionable
Drink, we could tell them
How much we liked them.

Happy the man who, dying, can
Place his hand on his heart and say:
'At least I didn't neglect to tell
The thrush how beautifully she sings.'

AT EIGHTY *Edwin Morgan*

Push the boat out, compañeros,
push the boat out, whatever the sea.
Who says we cannot guide ourselves
through the boiling reefs, black as they are,
the enemy of us all makes sure of it!
Mariners, keep good watch always
for that last passage of blue water
we have heard of and long to reach
(no matter if we cannot, no matter!)
in our eighty-year-old timbers
leaky and patched as they are but sweet
well seasoned with the scent of woods
long perished, serviceable still
in unarrested pungency
of salt and blistering sunlight. Out,
push it all out into the unknown!
Unknown is best, it beckons best,
like distant ships in mist, or bells
clanging ruthless from stormy buoys.

NOTES ABOUT THE POEMS

'Things' / Fleur Adcock
When the first line of this poem popped into my head it struck me as something people can identify with. I was pleased when the unnamed 'things'—our worst personal anxieties, whatever they may be—took on a life of their own. We all recognise them.

'The Unprofessionals' / Described by R. V. Bailey
U. A. Fanthorpe's poem is about what happened when our friends' son, who was at home, unwell, from university, suddenly vanished—along with the family car. The car was later found by a river, but there was never any trace of the boy. Apart from being with his parents, there was little that anyone could do. But they did what they could.

From: 'Doing Calls on the Old Portpatrick Road' / Iain Bamforth
'Graham's Landing' is part 12 of a 30-poem sequence based on my year as a trainee GP in Galloway in 1993. The way technologies uncouple the senses has always intrigued me: diagnostic acumen in medicine is so overwhelmingly *sighted*, while the face-to-face of the clinical encounter, at the beck and call of *hearing*, has come to seem archaic.

'White Basin' / Lindy Barbour
This poem was written on Lindisfarne, a decade after my mother's death from pancreatic cancer. After the diagnosis, she was able to return home, where I looked after her for three months. At such a time, everyday objects and surroundings become important and beautiful.

'A Brief Format...' / Glenn Colquhoun
I love the consultation. It is the high altar of medicine, God and

priest and man all in the same place at the same time, no-one knowing who is who and someone always roaming around. It strikes me how much is assumed within it and how most of the time those assumptions are accurate...most of the time.

'Teddy' / Glenn Colquhoun

I wrote this poem for a three-year-old patient with leukaemia. She screamed at her doctors whenever we entered her room on the ward. On Christmas Day Santa Claus gave her a water pistol. After that we were allowed in as long as we were shot one by one without mercy. She is well now and trains dogs. Water pistols should be a mainstay of cancer treatment.

'A medical education' / Glenn Colquhoun

I wrote the poems in *Playing God* as a young doctor and so many of my experiences in medicine were experiences I was having for the first time. I felt as though I was bobbing from flowerbed to flowerbed in some huge botanical garden. I was encountering the body as a character for the first time and learning that each part carried its own personality.

From 'Playing God' / Glenn Colquhoun

There is a great deal of medicine that doctors possess not because they have been to medical school but because they have lived life. They have been sons and daughters and mothers and fathers and friends and lovers. Sometimes it is the medicine these experiences teach us that is the most powerful of all.

'To My Surgeon' / Valerie Gillies

This poem recalls what it feels like to be the patient who hears that mammogram and biopsy have missed the cancer and that it has gone undetected for a long time. I owe my life to a surgeon who was sharp-eyed and persistent enough to diagnose this particular cancer.

'28 Weeks' / Lesley Glaister

Our grand-daughter Imogen was born by emergency caesarian at 28 weeks and her immediate prospects weren't very bright. Once she'd survived the first few weeks and was discharged from hospital we worried that some developmental problem might occur but by the time she was eighteen months, it was clear that she was perfectly, wonderfully fine.

'Ultrasound' / Kathleen Jamie

I loved the ultrasound image of my baby. Humans are very visual, we seem to have actually to see something to believe it. Also, I was interested in the relationship between sound and image. Ultrasound was non-invasive, exciting, confirming. But the grainy grey image made the baby seem like a ghost, a wee ghoul from the future, not the past. Not a scary ghost, but one you'd feel tender towards.

'Poem for a Hospital Wall' / Diana Hendry

This poem was written when I was writer-in-residence at Dumfries & Galloway Royal Infirmary. There was an artist working there too—Rachel Mimiec—and she wrote or painted the poem on a corridor wall of the hospital. We used the passages off as line breaks!

'Psalm Eighty-Eight Blues' / Diana Hendry

In an Oxfam bookshop, I found, Peter Hately Waddell's *The Psalms: Fra Hebrew intil Scottis*. I loved them. 'Psalm Eighty-Eight Blues' was prompted by the epigraph to Psalm 88 which reads 'A cry from the heart to God, neither light nor hopeful'. I think my poem is a prayer.

'Tools of The Trade' / Martin MacIntyre

I wrote 'Tools of The Trade' in response to the announcement of the bold plan to gift a collection of poems to newly graduated doctors in Scotland; I was delighted when it was accepted for this important book. Drawing on my own medical experience and that of others, I tried to convey the power of poetry to support, inform and re-humanise and its crucial place in the survival armoury of health professionals and their patients.

'Going Without Saying' / Bernard O'Donoghue
The poem was written after the death of a friend of mine—a successful industrial chemist in his 40s with a lovely wife and three children, who committed suicide totally unexpectedly. His devastated wife was partly comforted by a letter he left, saying how much he loved and admired her.

'Stroke haiku' / Helen Price
I wrote this haiku after having a stroke in May 2014, which left me with homonymous hemianopia and consequently unable to drive. I reckon that there are lots of benefits in not being able to drive—I have counted 67 to date. Many of the benefits are opportunities.

'Jackson Spander', selected by the editors from a public call, promoted by leading medical journals, for poem submissions / Described by Dr Alex Scott-Samuel, public health physician, Liverpool
Kenneth Dale Beernink was a brilliant young doctor who tragically died of chronic myelogenous leukaemia in 1969, four years after he graduated at Stanford University. During his internship at Yale and later at Stanford he wrote a series of case study poems featuring patients of all ages and a wide range of pathologies and social circumstances. They are all highly sensitive, deeply caring and beautifully crafted.

From 'A Year and a Day' / Described by Jill Turnbull
Gael was a good listener and observer of detail—essential to both his writing and doctoring. His spur-of-the-moment decision to record something heard, seen, or experienced every day for a year brings to life the resilience, humour, sorrow and strength of this patients and the small delights of the seasons.

'Daughter' / Ellen Bryant Voigt
In January 1975, the sore throat and fever of my 3-year old increased to the point that she refused to swallow anything. Alone in the house, I phoned a neighbor for a ride to the emergency room: I was carrying her downstairs when she stopped breathing and turned blue. She had acute epiglottitis, for which there is now, thankfully, a vaccine.

'Precious Ten Minutes' / Hamish Whyte
The poem is for my GP, Dr Ian Davey, who has looked after me with care and consideration since I moved to Edinburgh in 2004. Unfortunately he's now retired, but at least he'll have more time for his wonderful photographs of birds, some of which brightened up his surgery.

ACKNOWLEDGEMENTS

Our thanks are due to the following authors, publishers
and estates who have generously given permission
to reproduce works:

Dannie Abse, 'X-Ray' from *Ask the Moon* (Hutchinson, 2014),
reprinted by permission of The Random House Group Limited;
Fleur Adcock, 'Things' from *Poems 1960–2000* (Bloodaxe Books,
2000), by permission of the publisher; Patricia Beer, 'Recovery
Room' from *Autumn* (Carcanet Press, 1997), by permission of
the publisher; Iain Bamforth, 'Graham's Landing' from *Open
Workings* (Carcanet, 1996), by permission of the publisher; Lindy
Barbour, 'White Basin' from *Where You Start From* (Mariscat Press,
2015), by permission of the author; Wendell Berry, 'The Peace
of Wild Things' from *New Collected Poems* (Counterpoint, 2012)
Copyright © 2012 by Wendell Berry, reprinted by permission of
Counterpoint; Sarah Broom, 'Ward 64', from *Tigers at Awhitu*
(OxfordPoets / Carcanet Press, 2010), by permission of the
publisher; Rafael Campo, 'Iatrogenic' from *Alternative Medicine*
(Duke University Press, 2013) Copyright © by Rafael Campo.
Reprinted by permission of Georges Borchardt, Inc., for the
author; Raymond Carver, 'What the Doctor Said' from *All of Us*
(Harvill Press, 1997), reprinted by permission of The Random
House Group Limited; Arthur Cochrane, 'Mum', by permission
of the author; Glenn Colquhoun, 'A medical education', 'A brief
format to be used when consulting with patients', 'Teddy', and
'A note of warning to patients when all else fails', from *Playing
God: Poems about medicine* (Steele Roberts, 2002), by permission
of the publisher; Douglas Dunn, 'Second Opinion', from